Belle Vue

Manchester's Playground

at heart publications

Manchester
EveningNews

First published in 2007 by
At Heart Publications
32 Stamford Street, Altrincham, Cheshire, WA14 1EY
In conjunction with
Manchester Evening News
1 Scott Place, Hardman Street, Manchester, M3 3RN

ISBN 978-1-84547-164-4

Printed by Bell and Bain, Glasgow.

Introduction

The hardest part of writing this book has been the introduction. The problem is simple: how do you describe a community as exotic and diverse as Belle Vue Zoological Gardens? Belle Vue means more to its visitors and workers than historical facts can ever relay. It is a wondrous place consigned to people's memories and imagination.

Belle Vue Zoological Gardens was the creation of the entrepreneur John Jennison. Originally Jennison opened a small venture in Stockport known as the 'Strawberry Gardens' where he and his wife sold their produce and eventually developed a small aviary. From this initial concept, John Jennison developed the business and finally signed a lease on the Belle Vue site in 1836. The Jennison family were responsible for the expansion and initial development of the site. They took a disused lime pit and transformed it into world renowned zoological gardens that lasted beyond their family's involvement.

Under the management of the Jennison family, Belle Vue thrived, although it was not without its minor financial skirmishes, with John Jennison undergoing bankruptcy proceedings in 1843. Although attempts were made to sell the site it was eventually agreed by the creditors that they would see if Jennison could make a go of the Gardens and repay the loan. Within a relatively short period if time, John Jennison had paid his creditors their full entitlement.

The 1843 season also witnessed the Belle Vue site expansion and developments were underway to create a small lake, later renamed the Firework Lake. The Jennison family began to expand the zoological exhibits to include monkeys and bears. They also spent money in the development of the gardens to include beautiful fountains, grottos, a maze and eventually the individual gardens had a themed design to the layout.

After a visit to the Great Exhibition in London, Jennison returned with yet more ideas on how to develop Belle Vue. The results of the trip could be seen for many years afterwards in the beautiful and fantastic firework displays that Belle Vue became famous for. He hired George Danson as Belle Vue's scenic artist with one of his responsibilities being the 30,000 square foot canvas picture as the backdrop to his stunning fireworks. Jennison had envisioned a dramatic firework display that would incorporate a battle reenactment. This proved to be a very popular attraction at the Gardens and turned Belle Vue into an all day entertainment venue.

After John Jennison died in 1867, his family continued his vision into the next century. He had instilled in them his sense of self-sufficiency for Belle Vue's future, they baked their own bricks, brewed their own beer, printed their own guides, made their own fireworks and grew their own vegetables.

In 1925 the site was sold on to Belle Vue (Manchester) Ltd and John Henry Iles became the new Managing Director. During his directorship the Gardens expanded to include a new amusement park. The Fun Fair was one of the major attractions at Belle Vue even to the final closure of the site. With rides like the Bobs, Caterpillar, Scenic Railway, Water Chute, Merry-Go-Rounds, Go Karts and Elephant rides, Belle Vue became a world renowned amusement park.

Kings Hall was converted in 1928 so that it had a central stage area with seating circling round in tiers. The hall was used as a venue for a multitude of events including wrestling and boxing tournaments, musical events, brass band contests and the Christmas Circus. Ringmaster for the Christmas Circus in the initial 1929/30 season was George Lockhart, whose personality and showmanship made him a firm favourite with Belle Vue's visitors. Lockhart remained a regular feature of the Christmas Circus for 43 years.

Speedway was introduced to Belle Vue in 1928 but by March 1929, John Henry Iles had recognised its crowd-pulling potential and built a stadium for this new attraction next to the amusement park. Over the years the Aces team included members like Peter Craven, Frank Varey, Ivan Mauger and Bill Kitchen. The stadium was not designed solely for Speedway, in the centre of the stadium was a football pitch and later on the stadium was also used for the Stock Car Racing and even tennis tournaments.

In 1936 Belle Vue held its Centenary Celebrations. This involved a re-design of some of the amusement park, gardens and zoo exhibits. The most well known new feature was the floral clock with the Buddha statue placed on top. Behind the clock was a large Gibbon Cage and a new open air zoological exhibit called Monkey Mountain.

The war years were difficult for Belle Vue. Although restrictions were placed on the activities held at the park, it did remain open for the duration of the war. The grounds were used for military training and the exhibition halls, many of the restaurants and office spaces were all taken over by the military. The firework displays were cancelled and many of the rides in the fun fair were closed down. Belle Vue became home to animals from other zoos that had been forced to close. Unfortunately, due to the lack of availability of certain foods, some of the animals perished. The Christmas Circus continued but they were restricted to afternoon performances only. It was in 1942 that the Hallé Orchestra made its home in Kings Hall after the Free Trade Hall in Manchester was bombed.

After the war, Belle Vue seemed to go through a boom period seeing crowds of 250,000 over the Easter weekends. Gerald Iles was continuing to develop the zoo and gradually replaced the animals lost during the war years. His radio broadcast, 'Children's Hour', was increasingly popular and in 1951 he made his first TV appearance. Belle Vue Zoo was respected world-wide as a zoo that recognised the importance and quality of care given to their animals. Gerald Iles did many of the operations on the animals himself as local vets did not always have the same specialised knowledge. Belle Vue continued to inject a 'fun' element into the zoo exhibits – they publicised the feeding times for their animals and the hippos were a firm favourite along with the sea lions.

Belle Vue also suffered bouts of vandalism and burglary, which resulted in the death and disappearance of some of the animals. The last grand themed firework display, in the style that went back to the Jennison era, took place in 1956 – the theme was Robin Hood and his Merrie Men. Unfortunately this display was not a financial success and subsequent displays were never reorganised to this grandeur again. In 1958 Belle Vue suffered a serious fire which resulted in the complete destruction of the Pagoda Restaurant, the outdoor dancing platform, the fireworks viewing platform, the Tudor suite, the York and American bars, Baronial Hall, the staff canteen, five shops and the popular Café. Alongside the damage to the buildings was the very near destruction of some of the zoo's animals but, due to the quick response from firemen and Zoo workers, most of the animals were saved. One of the animal casualties was a 17-year-old lioness called Judy, who had become so distressed that she had to be shot.

In 1963 Belle Vue changed ownership and became part of Charles Forte's group. He continued to make improvements to the zoo but also spent more time developing the dining and exhibition halls at the park. Belle Vue had another fire that destroyed the Cumberland and Windermere Suites, the same blaze also destroyed part of the Speedway Stadium. Repairs were made at Speedway and within a year the Cumberland and Windermere Suites were re-built with the addition of a new suite called the Kendal Suite.

The late 1960s saw the number of visitors to Belle Vue begin to decline and the management seemed to invest less and less into the zoo and amusement park. The exhibition halls seemed to thrive as they used the area for pop and rock concerts, brass band contests and conferences. In 1971, one of Belle Vue 's most iconic landmarks was finally demolished – the Bobs. The cost of upkeep on the great rollercoaster was felt to be too high.

The end of an era was in sight and the closure of the zoo was finally announced in August 1977. New homes were found for most of the animals, some even found homes with their old keepers. However the main sale of the site did not occur until January 1981 when it was announced that Belle Vue would belong to Espley Tyas Development Group. The group in turn had agreed to sell a large portion of the land to Wimpey, a housing development company.

Forte struck a deal with the Espley Tyas Development Group, to honour all agreed commitments for events at Belle Vue for eighteen months after the sale of the site – this included the Christmas Circus. It was not long before the gates to Belle Vue finally closed and an era in Manchester history reached its conclusion.

Yet Belle Vue remains strong in the memories of the thousands of visitors and workers that passed through its doors. It is now a place of dreams and remembrances that are an intrinsic part of local legend.

One of the many official Belle Vue guides produced for the gardens. The first guide was printed in 1847 detailing the numerous attractions of the improved site. However it was 1856 before the guide books to the gardens became a regular feature, largely due to the introduction of a printing office at the site. Eventually all Belle Vue's promotional material, posters, guide books and menus were produced 'in house'.

Charles and Richard Jennison standing before the Indian Temple and Grotto in 1906. In the background, on the left of the picture, is the Jennison amusement area. Charles spent most of his time overseeing the botanical aspects of the gardens, while Richard was more comfortable looking after the many visitors that flocked to Belle Vue.

Richard Jennison has been described as having the least active role in the running of Belle Vue during the early years. He died in 1919, aged 82, the last of the seven Jennison brothers to pass away. After his death, sole ownership of the zoo finally passed onto the third generation of the Jennison family.

Exploring the Indian Temple and Grotto, John Jennison (right) began his working life as a silk weaver. His interest in botany and his unique drive for business established the Belle Vue Zoological Gardens as one of the world's premier family entertainment centres.

An external and internal photograph of Belle Vue
Prison. The prison was built on Hyde Road, West Gorton
in 1848. There were four sections to the prison, one of
the sections held female prisioners. The jail was not
a capital sentence prison - it mainly functioned as a
short term jail. However inmates and warders alike
could hear the dramatic Belle Vue firework displays
and even the howls of some of the zoo's inmates. In
1888 the Prison was declared unsafe due to damage
to the foundations caused by local mining operations.
It was finally demolished in 1890. In true Jennison
style, nothing was to be wasted and some of the jail's
building blocks were later used in the construction of
the rhino enclosure.

The Jennison family bought a chimpanzee called
Consul from Wombwell's travelling menagerie in 1893.
He proved to be a very popular addition to the zoo,
unfortunately he died just over a year later. Such was
his popularity at the zoo that the Jennison family felt it
imperative to find a replacement. Pictured here in his
familiar pose, on a tricycle playing a violin, is Consul II.

The Jennison family's interest in the botanical garden sections of Belle Vue has been well documented. They created a tradition of beautiful gardens and tropical hot plant houses that continued beyond their influence at the site. Pictured here is Leonard Williams, one time head gardener at Belle Vue, accompanied by a local railway beauty queen at a tree planting ceremony in the 1920s.

The Hyde Road entrance to Belle Vue, complete with the new blue and yellow turnstiles and a model triceratops. In the background is the old entrance and the Palm Court Bar.

A general advertisement featured in the Manchester Evening News for Belle Vue highlighting how many different attractions the gardens had to offer.

This Crossley Dominion TDD64 trolley bus made its debut in 1950 and served with Manchester Corporation, particularly along Hyde Road, past Belle Vue and to Ashton-under-Lyne.

Zoo

In many ways the concept for Belle Vue originated through the Jennisons' botanical and zoological interests. Originally John Jennison had a small aviary at his house in Adswood, Stockport. He and his wife established a small business around their strawberry gardens and bird exhibit, charging people a small amount to enter. When Jennison was approached about the Belle Vue site in Manchester, he recognised the potential for expansion of his small business and took on the lease.

John Jennison quickly expanded the zoological exhibits at Belle Vue with a winning combination of landscaped gardens and increasingly exotic animal exhibits. From modest beginnings the Jennison family created the foundations of Belle Vue Zoological Gardens.

By 1856 the Jennison family had added lions, rhinos, bears, gazelles and kangaroos to their collection. In 1872 they bought their famous elephant, Maharajah, who had made the journey from Edinburgh to Manchester by foot due to the fact he had destroyed the railway transportation he was supposed to use. Maharajah was not normally a violent animal and for many years he gave elephant rides to hundreds of children at Belle Vue Zoo.

After several years under the management of the Jennison family, control of Belle Vue Zoo passed on to a company called Belle Vue (Manchester) Ltd in 1925. The growth of the zoo declined in the first few years of the new company's control and it was not until Gerald Iles was appointed Zoological Superintendent that the zoo became rejuvenated. Gerald Iles was only 21 when he took this position at Belle Vue Zoo. He had just finished a degree in Zoology at Manchester University and willingly took up the challenge to turn the zoo around. Iles completed a research library, which in later years, through his own study and dedicated note taking, he added to himself. He became known as one of the leading authorities on exotic animal care and more often than not was the main surgeon if an animal fell ill.

It was during the 1936 Centenary celebrations that Gerald Iles was able to instigate more dynamic alterations for the zoo. Funds were made available to rejuvenate some of the tired looking exhibits and under this auspice Iles created the Gibbon Cage and Monkey Mountain. This was the year that also saw the purchase of two Tigons – Kliou and Maude. The brother and sister pair were bought from Dresden Zoo in Germany.

Gerald Iles also ensured that the Reptile House was extended and modernised. He recognised the need to generate extra revenue beyond the ticket price and launched a Zoo shop. However, despite Gerald Iles' drive and vision for the zoo, nothing could prepare him for the outbreak of war. Due to the majority of his staff being drafted into the military, Iles was left with a skeleton crew supported by volunteers. By 1940, the availability of food for the animals was dramatically reduced and resulted in deaths. For some animals other feed alternatives were found and they managed to survive. Belle Vue was one of the only zoos to remain open during the war years and they even took in evacuee animals from other zoos.

In 1946 the new Head Keeper, Matt Kelly, was employed to take over from James Craythorne. Kelly worked closely alongside Gerald Iles and was instrumental in ensuring the quality of the zoo. Gerald Iles instigated new avenues of publicity for the zoo when he began his radio programme, 'Children's Hour', with the BBC in Manchester. By 1951, Iles was also making television programmes and, each time, Belle Vue Zoo and its animals were promoted. Gerald Iles included some of the Belle Vue animals in the Christmas Circus, in a feature entitled 'Noah's Ark'.

The zoo and its animals proved to be a great attraction for visitors and many school trips and holidays were planned around the exciting exhibits. In 1956, control of Belle Vue passed into Sir Leslie Joseph's hands, however Iles remained as Superintendent at the Zoo. The Centenary Garden display was moved to make room for the famous Water Chute ride. The Gibbon Cage was redesigned slightly and moved between the ballroom and Elephant House and Monkey Mountain made way for a new Monkeyrama.

In October 1957, Gerald Iles finally left Belle Vue Zoo but his legacy of animal care and developments in their living environments remained. Iles was succeeded by William Wilson as Zoological Superintendent. One of Wilson's developments at Belle Vue Zoo was the ruminant enclosures, built in a mock Mexican adobe style where the Zebras and Ankole cattle were housed.

In 1961, William Wilson was relieved of his position as Superintendent, and in the interim period Matt Kelly, the Head Keeper, took on the role. It wasn't until 1962 that new Superintendent Raymond Legge was employed. Legge had previously worked in a similar role at Chester Zoo and Blackpool Zoo. He reintroduced a similar style of showmanship as Gerald Iles to the Zoo. He began a new attraction in July 1963, of a Chimps' Tea Party that proved to be a great attraction. In the same year improvements were made to the giraffe enclosure, new ostrich and emu paddocks were created and work on the new Great Ape House began.

Work to the new Aquarium and Reptile House was completed in 1964. The new house was sympathetically landscaped and attention to habitat detail was an intrinsic part of how the animals were displayed. In the main hall was a tropical forest section with a waterfall and large pool. Small birds flew inside the glass structure and as visitors stepped over the bridge they could view the alligators and crocodiles.

Belle Vue's last Superintendent, Peter Grayson, took over from Raymond Legge in 1971. The new owner, Charles Forte, seemed reluctant to invest in the zoo and the closure of Belle Vue suddenly seemed imminent. It would be a further six years before that announcement was to be made. Many of the animals found new homes with other zoos in the country and some of the snakes and other reptiles found homes with their keepers. It was a decision that was to see the heart of Belle Vue disappear.

Centenary Celebrations started in earnest at Belle Vue in 1936. The floral clock complete with a statue of Buddha was originally a centre-piece for the display, with a large gibbon cage directly behind it. However in 1957, when this image was taken, there had been a redevelopment of the site. The floral clock and gibbon cage were moved between the Ballroom and Elephant House and the new water chute took over the original site.

Peter Grayson joined Belle Vue in 1971 and was the zoo's last Superintendent before its closure. As pictured here, he would regularly give other animals a little exercise whilst going round the zoo.

Elephant rides were a popular attraction at Belle Vue for many years. One of the most familiar faces at Belle Vue was Phil Fernandez the elephant keeper. Phil was originally from Malaysia and was easily recognisable in his flamboyant Eastern robes; he first came to Belle Vue in 1921 with an Indian Elephant, Lil. In this photograph he is pictured leading another elephant, Mary.

Elephants were one of Belle Vue's major attractions, even if you did not have the opportunity to have an Elephant ride you could still enjoy watching them in their enclosures or view them in the Elephant House. The Elephant House was significantly altered in 1935/6 in time for the Centenary Celebrations. Originally each elephant had individual stalls which were a little cramped, but when the stalls were re-designed they were replaced with double stalls, large enough to comfortably fit two elephants and still offer them space to move around more. The old iron and oak post were replaced with short spikes and a moat. In the 1960s a large outdoor paddock was added which allowed the elephants greater freedom.

Marty (left) and Mavis, Belle Vue's pygmy hippos. Pygmy hippos can have a life-span of 30-40 years and generally weigh between 400-500 pounds. Their bodies are almost entirely hairless, but to protect their skin and to keep it moist they secrete a clear mucus. When they are born, pygmy hippos are unable to swim until they are taught. When the zoo finally closed, Marty and Mavis were sold to Bristol Zoo where they continued to breed successfully in captivity.

Originally built in 1906, this outdoor pool serviced the hippos until 1969 when the new Tropical River House was erected. Keepers used to feed the hippos with whole loaves of bread, much to the astonishment of the spectators.

Taking a last dip in his pool, Hercules was one of the last hippos to reside at Belle Vue before its closure. Born at Whipsnade Zoo, in Bedfordshire, Hercules was later sold to Cleethorpes Zoo. When Cleethorpes closed he was moved on to to Dudley Zoo in the West Midlands where he eventually died of peritonitis.

Gerald Iles was a zoological Superintendant at Belle Vue from 1933 to 1957. He is pictured here taking part in a 'Children's Hour' broadcast at the BBC's Manchesterstudios. He was passionate about raising Belle Vue's profile as one of the leading zoos for the care and study of animals. He used to peform the majority of surgical operations on the animals himself, as the local vets of the time had little or insufficient knowledge about the care and physiology of exotic animals.

The Jennison family were the first owners of Belle Vue to introduce the Giraffes as a zoo attraction in 1871. However it was 1937 before the first Giraffe was born at Belle Vue. In the late 1950s, when this photograph was taken, the new zoological Superintendent, William Wilson, proposed that new enclosures needed to be built for the giraffes and camels.

The giraffe enclosure always proved to be a popular attraction at Belle Vue. Only a year after this photograph was taken in 1937, George and Mary had successfully produced a calf, Doreen, who spent many years at the zoo.

Addie the giraffe was very keen to see the Zoo's newest arrival - Monty, the baby zebra, born on Cup Final day 1973, and named after Sunderland's "man of the match" goal keeper, Jim Montgomery.

The addition of Zeek the Zebra to Belle Vue Zoo caused some excitement among the children of Richmond Infants School in Oldham, as they got to pick the baby zebra's name.

A familiar sight in 1937 as Belle Vue visitors are given a llama ride round the park.

Alongside the more exotic animals, Belle Vue was also home to more familiar residents. People would bring family pets that they could no longer look after to join the Zoo's menagerie, as seen here as a little girl bids a fond farewell to her pet duck.

One of Belle Vue's more famous faces, Matt Kelly, the longest serving Head Keeper at the zoo. He joined Belle Vue from Dublin Zoo in 1946 and did not retire until 1975. Kelly also occasionally filled the role of 'Acting Director' just until new Superintendents could be found. He is pictured here in 1968 with Perry the Peacock. Perry had led everyone a chase as he escaped into the Gorton streets around the zoo.

Posing for the cameras is ten-day-old Penny the Pigtailed Macaque. The zoo was home to a varied and unique collection of monkeys and apes.

The Zoo and Amusement Park were always intrinsically linked and this photograph highlights the unique balance that existed between the attractions at Belle Vue. The Miniature Railway was relocated and renamed the Santa Fe Railway. The locomotives were restyled in an American design and approximately £8,000 was spent on new lion and tiger enclosures and a 'Wolf Wood'. These Canadian Timber Wolves were eventually sold to Cleethorpes Zoo when Belle Vue closed.

Peter Grayson with Topaz the chimpanzee and Luke the Leopard. Many of the animals at Belle Vue Zoo had to be hand-reared due to the death or rejection of their mothers.

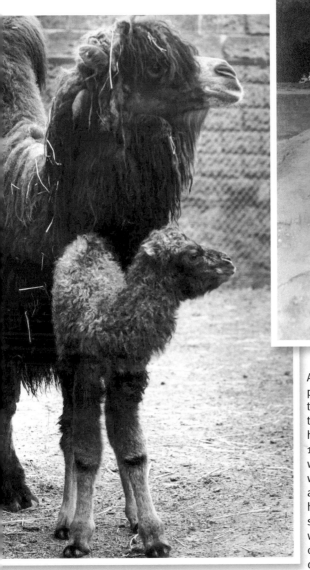

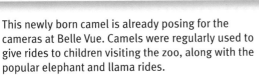

Asiatic Black Bears are particularly distinctive due to the cream coloured V-patch on their fur. Initially the bears were housed in pits or cages but in 1960 dramatic improvements were instigated. The new area was formed in terraces with rocks and pools so the bears could have more room to play. Even the sleeping quarters were designed with under-floor heating in order to make the bears more comfortable in their new home.

This newly born camel is already posing for the cameras at Belle Vue. Camels were regularly used to give rides to children visiting the zoo, along with the popular elephant and llama rides.

This young polar bear was rejected by its mother at birth. A wife of one of Belle Vue's executives took the cub to her home for four months and reared it herself. This photograph was taken when the young polar bear was reintroduced to the pool at Belle Vue.

Polar Bears were an intrinsic feature of the zoo even in the Jennison era. The first Polar Bear cage was constructed in 1855, eventually this was modernised by Gerald Iles in 1938. The next transformation of the Polar Bear enclosure occurred in 1960 when the whole section was remodelled as the Bear Terrace. The Polar Bears had more space with which to move around in, a more interesting terrain made up of rocks, pools and a moat. The old cage was not initially dismantled, in fact it was re-used temporarily as a lion enclosure.

In 1964, new larger enclosures were built for the big cats on the old site of the Jennison Bear Pits. A male lion in captivity has a life expectancy of 25-30 years and can weigh 450 pounds on average.

Seen here holding two tiger cubs is Belle Vue's last Zoo Superintendent, Peter Grayson. He used to take home many animals who needed specialised care or had been rejected by their parents.

Laurence Baker worked for 40 years as keeper of the lions and tigers at Belle Vue Zoo. He is pictured saying goodbye to the big cats he cared for as the news of the Zoo's closure is confirmed.

Rita the Tigon was a resident at Belle Vue from July 1957 to
February 1968. Originally owned by the Sultan of Morocco, she
was six years old when she arrived at Belle Vue Zoo from the
Vincennes Zoo, Paris.

Deserted by its mother, Blanca was adopted by an unusual surrogate family of Afghan hounds. The Tait family reared Blanca until the cub was old enough to return to Belle Vue Zoo.

One of a trio of lion cubs born to Jason and Sally in the late 1970s. When the zoo closed most of the lions were moved to Cleethorpes Zoo, except for one of the new cubs who was sent to Knaresborough Zoo in North Yorkshire.

John Christy was Head Zoo Keeper at Belle Vue when the zoo closed. Here he is pictured with one of the young lion cubs.

Peter Grayson (Zoological Superintendent) and Blanco, a hand reared Belle Vue lion. Grayson used to walk Blanco around the zoo on a regular basis, sometimes he even took him for a stroll down Hyde Road, Gorton.

Relaxing in the sun is one of Belle Vue's cheetahs. We are not entirely sure if this is Stookie or Don Jose. At this time Belle Vue also had a female cheetah, Michaela, purchased from Ceylon, Sri Lanka.

Winston Taylor was the curator of the Aquarium and Reptile House at Belle Vue for over 40 years. During his time at Belle Vue, Winston witnessed many additions to the Reptile House, several of these arriving through less conventional routes in the packing for the fruit and vegetables at Smithfield market.

Funfair

Funfairs have always held a magical element for children and adults, due in part to the total absorption of the visitor in having fun. Belle Vue was no exception to this maxim, if anything it managed to exceed it. The electrifying combination of funfair rides, animal rides, restaurants and food stalls, botanical gardens, firework displays, boating lakes and dancing was unrivalled. The close links with the Zoo and other musical and sporting attractions meant that there was something to appeal to the entire family.

Originally the emphasis was placed on the zoological and botanical aspects of Belle Vue. The Jennison family developed beautiful gardens with fountains, arbours, a maze based on the one at Hampton Court, Lakes, Grottos, flower-beds and even a bowling green. On the lakes they had rowing boats and even paddle steamers which visitors could either hire or take a relaxing trip around the lake on. A large wooden open air dancing area was located next to the lake where in the evenings amazing firework displays were put on. Many of the displays were battle re-enactments, they included the famous large 'Picture' backdrop, cannon fire and hundreds of men as actors in the skirmishes.

The Zoo and the Funfair were always closely linked, especially with the theatrical elements, to the presentation of some of the animals. The elephant rides were always a popular attraction for visitors to Belle Vue, along with the Chimpanzee Tea-Parties and Consul (a tricycle riding, Violin playing Chimpanzee). Children also were able to take camel and llama rides through the grounds.

Although there was a limited selection of funfair rides at Belle Vue during the Jennison family's ownership of the park, it was an element of the centre that they failed to develop fully. When ownership of the Gardens transferred to 'Belle Vue (Manchester) Ltd', there was a distinctive shift towards the provision of funfair rides.

John Henry Iles became Belle Vue's Managing Director in 1925 and instigated many new developments in his first year. Some of the new rides Iles introduced that year include the Caterpillar, Jack & Jill, the Dodgems, the Flying Sea Planes, Ghost Train and the famous Scenic Railway. Although the Scenic Railway was bought in 1925 it was not fully functional until 1927. It remained one of Belle Vue's all-time greatest rides replacing the figure 8 Toboggan and stayed in use until 1975.

The Bobs was arguably the most well-known ride at Belle Vue, given this nickname because it cost a shilling to ride it. It was purchased from Fred Church and Tom Prior who had developed new engineering innovations that made the exciting ride possible. It was an 80 ft high drop at a 45 degree angle and went at a speed of a mile a minute. Not only was the ride a thrilling burst of speed and excitement but its structure dominated the Belle Vue skyline.

During the Second World War, some of the amusement rides like the Flying Sea Planes were closed and the number of rides allowed to operate at this time was restricted to just ten. Belle Vue as an amusement park did remain open during the war years and servicemen were admitted at half the price.

The Post-war boom years at Belle Vue was reflected in the emergence of new rides and attractions at the funfair, most noticeably the Water Chute. When the funfair finally closed, the Water Chute ride was bought by Blackpool Pleasure Beach and re-named 'Vikingar'.

Belle Vue also offered a varied selection of places to eat, anything from a fish and chip shop or an ice-cream shop to a licensed restaurant like the Palm Court. Many people used to take a picnic or packed lunch to eat in the gardens. The food service industry was always an important factor at Belle Vue, instigated largely by the Jennison Family. At one time, Belle Vue grew its own vegetables, had its own brewery and had a bakery.

A 1950s advertisement for the popular Water Chute ride.

Passengers taking the plunge on the Water Chute, at Belle Vue in the 1960s.

Workmen are seen checking the track of the Water Chute. This is the view passengers would have seen as they made their descent into the water below. This Water Chute was built in 1957 and replaced a more primitive ride.

A couple enjoy the thrill of
Belle Vue's Water Chute.

The Helter Skelter Lighthouse was originally built in 1906 next to the small lake. The building to the left of the Helter Skelter is Belle Vue's electrical installation.

The Miniature Railway was developed at Belle Vue in 1928 and originally ran in a straight line along the Avenue. Over the years it was developed into a loop-line and finally got relocated and renamed as the Santa Fe Railway. Standing just in front is the Helter Skelter which children could ride for 6d a go.

A familiar sight as children wait impatiently for their turn on the Merry-Go-Round.

The Ferris Wheel at Belle Vue allowed people to have a more leisurely view over the funfair and also proved to be a particular attraction for young couples.

During World War Two, many of Belle Vue's grounds and buildings were utilised for training purposes in the war effort. Pictured here are two factory girls learning about a Bren gun at Belle Vue. The war meant that many of the Belle Vue workers were called into military service and retired former keepers were drafted in to care for the animals. Belle Vue remained open for business during the war, except for a two week period. However, the normal opening hours were reduced. The Christmas Circus continued although many of the normal acts could not be included as travel in Europe was severely restricted.

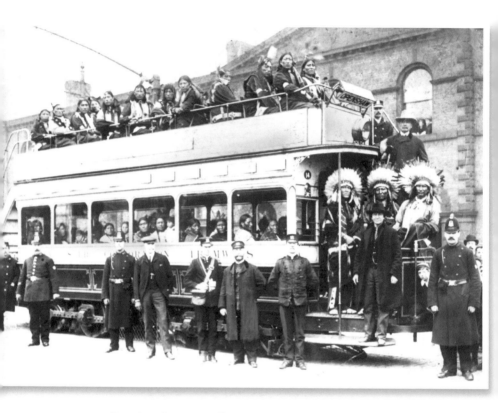

On a day trip out to Belle Vue is
a company of unique visitors.
Photographed outside the main
entrance is 'Buffalo Bill' Cody with
his Wild West Show. He toured
throughout Europe performing with
familiar names such as Chief Sitting
Bull and Annie Oakley.

A popular amusement at Belle Vue was the smaller boating lake where you could take a ride on either a rowing or motor boat. Salford suffered serious flooding in 1946 so Belle Vue's rowing boats were recruited to get people to safety.

Belle Vue was devastated by a major fire in January 1958. The blaze had already taken hold before the fire department could reach the site. Instead, the firemen did all that they could to save the animals housed nearby whilst limiting the damage that had already occurred to the buildings.

The 1958 blaze was so intense that it consumed the ballroom, cafes, shops, bars, and the Jennison firework viewing platform. The fire had raged so strongly that it had reached within a foot of the Lion House and if the local fire department had not made such heroic efforts, much more would have been lost.

More devastation from the 1958 fire. Here the destruction of the Pagoda Restaurant, Gallery Bar and Staff Canteen are apparent. It also shows how close the fire came to destroying the Lion House. Unfortunately one of the older lionesses, Judy, became very distressed and the keepers found it necessary to shoot her.

The full devastation of the 1958 fire was not realised until the following morning. Spectators begin to gather at the site of the York Restaurant and Coronation Ballroom.

Valuable circus equipment was destroyed in a blaze at the banqueting suites. Other equipment lost included the new £1,500 coconut mat used in the Kings Hall arena.

Tangled metal and charred woodwork mark what was once the entrance to the Cumberland and Windermere Suites after the fire of 1964.

Flat caps and bowler hats for the men and straw boaters for the girls! This 1900 photograph shows the open air dancing area and the Lighthouse Café is on the left of the picture. On the right is a paddle steamer which used to carry passengers on the Firework Lake. Behind the boat is part of the 'Large Picture'. It measured nearly 30,000 square feet and was used as a backdrop for the fantastic firework displays. The original 'Large Picture' was painted by Belle Vue's own scenic artist George Danson. Instigated by the Jennison family, they erected a large 4,000 seater, elevated gallery as a viewing platform for spectators.

Some of the cast of a Belle Vue Firework spectacular. A closer look at the "ladies" on the mobile contraption reveals stiff collars, ties and remarkably masculine faces.

Belle Vue's dramatic firework displays were usually accompanied by battle re-enactments. Belle Vue used local people as extras in the displays, photographed here are members of the American Civil War Society with guns at the ready.

David Lloyd George addresses a huge crowd at Belle Vue in 1924. Lloyd George was actually born in Manchester on 17 January 1863. His father, a schoolmaster, died a year later and his mother took her two children to live with her brother in Wales. Lloyd George joined the Liberal Party and became an MP in 1890. His dramatic oratory quickly brought him to the attention of the leaders of the Liberal Party, eventually becoming Prime Minister of a coalition government during WWI.

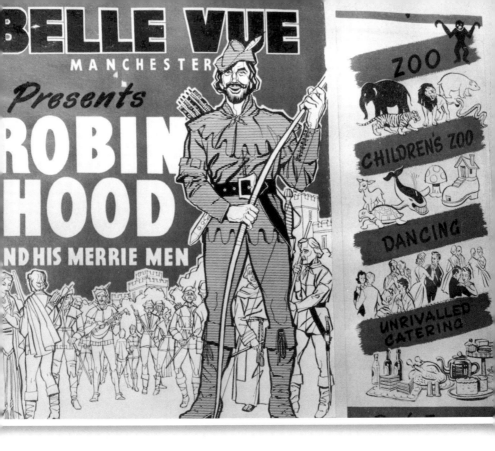

An advertisment for Belle Vue's final large firework display, Robin Hood and his Merrie Men, in 1956. From then on, Belle Vue's firework displays were less flamboyant.

The Chinese Café at Belle Vue was incredibly popular with visitors. The brightly coloured Chinese lanterns, parasols and painted walls were in stark relief against the starch Victorian dress of the waitresses. The Jennisons originally decorated the café in this fashion in 1889 and it remained in this style for many years.

There were many events held at Belle Vue over the years, including animal shows like this dog show pictured here.

The Lake Hotel Belle Vue pictured in 1971 on the junction of Hyde Road, Mount Road and Kirkmanshulme Lane. The local landmark was opened in 1876 but eventually it was destroyed by fire.

On the right of the photograph is the popular Go-Kart track and in the background the famous Scenic Railway. The Scenic Railway replaced the Figure 8 Toboggan in 1926, the ride finally closed in 1975.

The Figure 8 Toboggan was installed at Belle Vue in 1908 and was located between a maze and the Paddock. It was installed in the grounds after James Jennison witnessed one in action at White City, Stretford. The ride was finally replaced by the Scenic Railway.

Belle Vue in the late 1950s as these young children pose for the camera. In the background is one of the funfairs merry-go-rounds and the back of the Scenic Railway.

The Bobs serves as a dramatic backdrop to another famous Belle Vue ride, the Caterpillar. The Caterpillar ran on a wave-like track with the cars getting faster and faster as they went round the track. A canopy fell over the car, plunging the passengers into darkness. From the outside, the moving cars resembled a green caterpillar.

The dominant framework of The Bobs looms in the background of this family snapshot. The Bobs was originally opened in 1929 and, at 80 feet in height, it was a considerable distance to plunge down again!

Circus

The annual Christmas Circus was an institution in the region for many years, bringing excitement and wonder to the countless people who sat enthralled under its big top. The circus at Belle Vue was amongst the finest in Europe, there was no expense spared in recruiting the best acts and ensuring that the fans always had an amazing time.

The first circus to be held at Belle Vue was in 1922, but it was not a successful venture and the idea was put on hold for a few years. In December 1929, the director of the Zoo, Gerald Iles, and his father, William, collaborated with Alderman Tom Bickerstaff of the Blackpool Tower Company over the transfer of much of the Blackpool circus acts and equipment to Belle Vue. An early transfer between the two was a man that achieved legendary status and will forever be linked with Belle Vue's triumphant past, George Lockhart.

Lockhart, known as the "Prince of Ringmasters", reigned at Belle Vue Circus for an unbelievable 43 years. His personality left an indelible mark over the entire operation and his face adorned countless posters; he was as much part of the circus as the Kings Hall itself. In fact, for the 1967/68 season which marked his 39th consecutive year at Belle Vue, the circus was renamed the "George Lockhart Celebration Circus" in his honour. George Lockhart unfortunately passed away in 1979, but his memory lives on. A name forever linked with George Lockhart in the history of Belle Vue Circus is Fred Bonelli. As a young boy, Fred had played trumpet with Barnum and Bailey's Band and went on to become a great bandleader. He conducted the bands in Belle Vue for over thirty years and was an integral part of the spectacle.

During the Second World War, Lockhart was put in sole charge of the circus. Under his leadership, Belle Vue managed to stage the shows, even under intense pressure. There was a severe lack of acts and staff, as well as limits on when the performances could actually take place. During the Blitz, night-time performances were stopped altogether. But the show did go on, and even through all the hardship, Belle Vue Circus was a ray of hope, giving people much-needed happiness and enjoyment during hard times.

Over the years there were hundreds of acts that performed in the Kings Hall. They travelled from every corner of the globe in order to thrill the crowds who flocked into Belle Vue every Christmas. The extensive journey around Europe to find the best acts was a time consuming one, usually undertaken by the management of the circus.

Entertainment in the circus was not just about people though. There were also many animals that played a part in the success of Belle Vue Circus. Performing sea lions, tigers, elephants, polar bears, dogs, birds, horses and a whole host of other creatures ensured that the circus remained colourful, energetic and entertaining. Many people assumed that the animals they saw performing were simply "borrowed" from the zoo for a few hours, but that was not the case at all. An exception to this rule however, was the sea lions. Evelyn and "Captain" Harry Schmidt trained these animals extensively, and they gave performances both in the circus and inside the confines of the zoo. The other exception was under Gerald Iles' leadership, when he staged his Belle Vue 'Noah's Ark' feature.

Clowns have a vital role in the circus, and Belle Vue had its fair share, from Tambo and Tambo, Ross and Willie, Ross Adam, Johnco and of course Jacko Fossett. Jacko caused mayhem and humour for over thirty years in the Kings Hall with his partner Little Billy Merchant always by his side.

The job of taking over as Ringmaster after the departure of George Lockhart was a difficult task. But Norman Barrett, a man with a long history in the circus, took the job and stamped his own impression on the Belle Vue public. He was a commanding presence in the big top, and garnered the respect of all the performers and staff. It was Barrett who presided over the last circus to take place in the Kings Hall in 1981.

Although efforts were made to keep the circus going, with performances being staged in the car park and in a tent on Hyde Road, it was the destruction of the Kings Hall that really signalled the end for Belle Vue Circus.

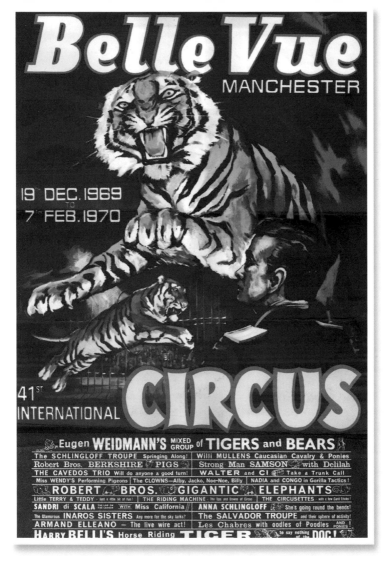

Belle Vue
MANCHESTER

19 DEC. 1969
TO
7 FEB. 1970

41ST INTERNATIONAL CIRCUS

Eugen **WEIDMANN'S** MIXED GROUP of **TIGERS** and **BEARS**

The SCHLINGLOFF TROUPE Springing Along!	Willi MULLENS Caucasian Cavalry & Ponies
Robert Bros. BERKSHIRE PIGS	Strong Man SAMSON with Delilah
THE CAVEDOS TRIO Will do anyone a good turn!	WALTER and CI Take a Trunk Call
Miss WENDY'S Performing Pigeons	The CLOWNS—Alby, Jacko, Noe-Noe, Billy	NADIA and CONGO in Gorilla Tactics !

ROBERT BROS. GIGANTIC ELEPHANTS

Little TERRY & TEDDY — Just a little bit of Fun!	THE RIDING MACHINE - The Ups and Downs of Circus	THE CIRCUSETTES - with a few Card Tricks !
SANDRI di SCALA THE LAD ON THE LADDER WITH Miss California	ANNA SCHLINGLOFF She's going round the bends!
The Glamorous INAROS SISTERS Any more for the sky larks!	The SALVADOR TROUPE and their sphere of activity!
ARMAND ELLEANO — The live wire act!	Les Chabres with oodles of Poodles AND PONIES !

HARRY BELLI'S Horse Riding TIGER to say nothing of the DOG!

The Christmas Circus was a tradition at Belle Vue that carried on for many years. This advertisement for the 41st International Circus in the 1969/70 season had quite a line-up of acts. At the bottom of the poster is 'Harry Belli's Horse Riding Tiger : to say nothing of the dog!' Harry Belli ran his own small circus in Holland and the act mentioned here includes a tiger called Byla, his horse Bulle and the dog Jimmy.

Jacko Fossett with Maureen, one of the Robert Brothers' Circus elephants. Jacko worked with the Robert Brothers' Circus for many years until he joined the Mill's Circus in 1962.

Robert Fossett, better known as Jacko the Clown, outside Belle Vue Circus. Jacko started his circus career as a trapeze artist along with his three sisters. Partnered with fellow clown, Little Billy Merchant, for almost three decades they were a popular duo at the circus.

Leading her team of two horses is one of Robert Brothers' Circus riders. She is already dressed in her costume ready for the evening performance in the main exhibition hall.

Trainer Brenda Hani in one of her Indian Elephant Acts at Belle Vue Circus. There were many other Elephant tricks and acts performed regularly at the circus.

The Bogino Brothers performing at Belle Vue to an admiring crowd. While one brother juggles in the background the other balances skilfully across the handlebars and seat of the moving bicycle whilst saluting the crowd.

Thorson Kohrmann and his Farmyard Friends Act at Belle Vue Circus. In the background the pig looks a little bored to see the goat leaping fences.

The audience gets a good soaking as Jacko the clown's hat squirts out water over people too near the ring.

The 'Trio Biarge' were a family of jugglers who came from Spain to perform at Belle Vue. Saluting her two 'spinning' brothers is Esmerelda Briattori. She had contracted polio as a child and it had left her with a withered leg. This however did not hinder her performance.

Will Jacko be able to quench the flames emerging from his fellow clown's hat in time?

Husband and wife act, Los Alamos, performing their popular hatchet trick for a rapt Belle Vue audience. Tensions were high, especially because Rolf was blindfolded!

Rev. J.A. Carr christening a new
addition to the Belle Vue Circus family
with Jacko the Clown as godfather.

Jacko Fossett without his clown apparel sitting in Kings Hall for the last time before it was demolished. Although the Christmas Circus did continue for a few more seasons it was no longer performed within the famous hall.

The Circus played in the Kings Hall for many years along with other sporting and musical performances. Although many of the Circus acts could perform with ease, the flying trapeze and high wire acts were unable to perform due to the restricted height of the hall.

Santa Claus returns to Manchester to let people know that although Belle Vue has closed, the traditional Christmas Circus will go on. In the background the demolition of Kings Hall continues but lined up in front are some of Belle Vue Circus' most famous faces including Jacko Fossett.

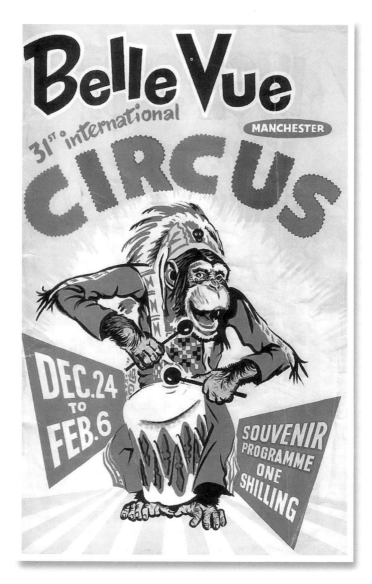

This souvenir programme for Belle Vue's 31st
International Circus was sold for only one shilling.

Music

When people recall Belle Vue in its prime, one of the first things that will come to mind is the music. Whether it was ballroom dancing, brass bands, pop concerts or classical music, Belle Vue was a place where one could always be sure to hear a great tune.

As early as 1851, a Ballroom was situated above the Longsight entrance to the park. Another musical innovation was the Brass Band Contests that started in 1853. John Jennison had seen the benefits of musical competitions when he visited the Great Exhibition at the Crystal Palace, London, and decided that Belle Vue's own Brass Band was being under-used. This led to the implementation of a trial contest in 1852, which proved a huge success.

It was during the 1860s that another legendary feature of Belle Vue was created, with the building of an outdoor dancing platform. This wooden landmark was enjoyed by generations of folks who met, danced and fell in love in the open air. The dance floor remained in use up until 1958, although it had become used as a roller skating rink after the Second World War.

During the late years of the 19th Century, the popularity of the Brass Band and other musical contests had continued to grow. In 1886, a second Brass Band contest was introduced into the Belle Vue calendar and in 1900 a series of Military Band contests took place for the first time.

In the 1930s, efforts were made to bring the whole park up-to-date; which included a complete remodelling of the Kings Hall at a price of £30,000. This turned the venue from a basic hall to the all-seated arena that most people remember. It allowed the venue to host a large variety of performances, including jazz, popular music and big bands. Also, the venue was used to host various rallies, meetings and of course the Circus.

The war years proved as tough for Belle Vue as it did for the rest of the country, with large parts of the grounds being used by the army for training and manufacture. The Hallé Orchestra began to use the Kings Hall in the 1940s, after their original home was destroyed during the Blitz. This was the beginning of a long and fruitful association with Belle Vue that lasted over thirty years.

Although the Brass Band competitions experienced a gradual decline in popularity during the 1960s, things picked up with the re-emergence of the competitions due to increased exposure, particularly on television and in schools, and the sights and sounds particular to Brass Band music were often experienced inside the Kings Hall.

Belle Vue continued to be a popular venue for all manner of concerts well into the 1970s, with huge names such as Jimi Hendrix, The Who, The Rolling Stones, and Led Zeppelin all making appearances. The Kings Hall remained one of the region's best venues for live music, with seating for 5,000 and great acoustics.

The slow and sad demise of Belle Vue as the North West's premier leisure attraction and music venue meant the area was robbed of a vital part of its heritage. Following the closure of the zoo, plans were made to redevelop the rest of the park, including the Kings Hall. All of the exhibitions venues were sold to the Espley Tyas Development Group who agreed to honour all existing contracts over the next 18 months.

This announcement created a new wave of protest from people who had enjoyed the Kings Hall and those who used it for exhibitions and concerts. Action groups were formed and 50,000 people signed a petition in an attempt to block the sale. Some of the opponents formed their own development company that devised a new scheme more in fitting with Belle Vue's original usage, but unfortunately their efforts proved to be in vain.

The final event to be staged inside the Kings Hall was the North West Amateur Brass Band Championship, on 14 February 1982. The actual demolition of the site had been delayed in order to ensure that this competition could take place. On this final occasion, 56 bands took part and over 1,700 people performed. It seemed a fitting finale to all those spectacular evenings in the Kings Hall down the years.

As with much of Belle Vue, the Kings Hall has a place in the hearts of countless people, both local and international. So many memories were demolished with it. Thousands who enjoyed wonderful nights of music within its walls are still mourning the loss of a legendary venue.

The venue was built over a six week period in 1910 in order to stage "Demonstrations, Exhibitions, Social Gatherings, etc". The Kings Hall was chosen to honour the two Kings in whose reign the construction fell within; George V and Edward VII.

An empty Belle Vue Ballroom. The original site of the Ballroom was above the main gateway to the park and held up to 500 people. But the original building was demolished in the 1950s after it was found to be in a dangerous condition.

Sixties pop group the Dave Clarke Five, one of the most successful bands in the 1960s. They ran neck-and-neck with The Beatles for a brief period and had eight Top Ten records between 1964-67. The band enjoyed great success on both sides of the Atlantic, as British music dominated the world.

A fan faints as the crowd goes crazy during a David Cassidy concert at Belle Vue in March 1973. A whole host of popular musical artists appeared in the Kings Hall through the years, including the Rolling Stones, The Who, Jimi Hendrix, The Beatles, Jerry Lee Lewis and The Clash.

Screaming Bay City Rollers fans are held back by Belle Vue security men as they attempt to reach the stage. It was during the 1960s that Belle Vue made the decision to embrace the popular music of the time with the start of the Top Ten Club, hosted by Jimmy Savile. This venture began in 1963 and grew large crowds of young people to Belle Vue.

Les McKeown of the Bay City Rollers singing on stage in the Kings Hall. The Bay City Rollers became wildly popular during the 70s, even if their fame only lasted a few years. The band chose their name after deciding they needed an American sounding one, and so stuck a pin in a map!

It wasn't only the crooners and well behaved pop acts that appeared at Belle Vue! Here is a great image of punk pop group The Clash, pictured after trouble flared up in the crowd during their Belle Vue concert.

The floor of the Elizabethan Suite was strewn with debris after trouble flared up as The Clash played to an "energetic" audience. It was quite rare for the Kings Hall to experience trouble of this kind, but punk music seemed to take trouble wherever it went.

Boys of Chetham's Hospital Choir rehearse outside their school for a British Legion Rememberance Service that was held at Belle Vue. Chetham's School of Music has a long association with Belle Vue. In fact, many of the original documents belonging to the Jennison family are still stored within Chetham's Library.

It wasn't just British stars thrilling the packed crowds inside the Kings Hall. Here is Bing Crosby pictured in September 1977 alongside Roy Chapel, a local crooner who sang in his style. Crosby enjoyed incredible popularity throughout the war, and proved a great guest for Belle Vue.

Star names made an impression on demolition workers at Belle Vue. The "Wall of Fame" was based in the Elizabethan Suite and featured imprints of the hands and feet of stars such as Bing Crosby, Pele, Omar Sharif and Gracie Fields.

Gracie Fields was a returning face at Belle Vue throughout the years. She is pictured here during one of the many exhibitions she attended. As early as 1936, Miss Fields opened the new aquarium. She was also present at the inauguration of the "Wall of Fame" attraction, pictured above.

It was left to the Glossop School Band to play the last ever piece of music to be heard in the Kings Hall. They were taking part in the North-West Amateur Brass Band Championship, held on 14 February 1982. Because of a fire at Bolton Town Hall, the concert was moved to Belle Vue, where the demolition of Kings Hall was delayed in order to accommodate it.

Sport

Sport always played an important part in the popularity of Belle View. Whether it was speedway, football, boxing or wrestling, the crowds flocked into the park in order to experience the pleasures that only sporting spectaculars can supply.

As early as 1847, sport began to play a part in Belle Vue's history, when a racecourse was added to the early site. This particular venture proved unsuccessful but it laid the foundation for many more sporting facilities and events that enthralled the public for over a hundred years.

It was in 1887 that sporting events really found a permanent base in Belle Vue as the Jennison family built an Athletic Ground near Hunters Lane. This stadium was looked on so favourably that Manchester City F.C were in negotiations with Belle Vue over the possible lease of this stadium to replace their Hyde Road site which had been decimated by fire. The discussions eventually proved unproductive, however, with the club eventually moving to Maine Road in 1923.

When the new company, Belle Vue (Manchester) Ltd, gained control of the park in 1925, a new wave of investment flooded into almost every aspect of the site. Control of this new company was in the hands of three men, Sir William Gentle, Captain J.P Hodge and John Henry Iles. It was Gentle and Hodge who set up the first Greyhound Stadium in the country on land leased from Belle Vue. They both eventually left the company in order to concentrate their interests on this new sport.

That left the control of Belle Vue down to John Henry Iles. One of the first things he did was to bring speedway back on to the park, at first using the Greyhound Track and Athletic Ground, which opened in 1929. Belle Vue's speedway team, the "Aces", went on to acquire a reputation as one of the most famous teams in the world, and the track has gone down in history as one of speedway's finest ever venues.

Iles instigated a number of sports that used the new stadium as their home with various degree of success. Rugby Union, baseball, chariot racing and tennis were all housed in the Speedway Stadium without making much of a real impact, but they all provided enjoyment to the crowds thirsty for a new spectacle.

Wrestling and boxing began to come to prominence in the 1930s after the Kings Hall had been given a face-lift, turning it into a fine arena capable of holding 5,000 people. The first wrestling contest was held in the Kings Hall on 15 December 1930 and featured Bert Assirati and Atholl Oakley. By the late thirties, Belle Vue had become a mecca for wrestling fans thrilled by the spectacle.

Many aspects of Belle Vue suffered during the Second World War, but speedway achieved the incredible feat of operating throughout, making do with riders on leave and great youngsters to give the public a much-needed lift in morale. The fifties saw the introduction of stock car racing from America as well as the continuation of speedway, wrestling and greyhound racing as mainstays of Belle Vue's appeal. Broughton Rangers, Belle Vue's resident football team, were given a new start as Belle Vue Rangers F.C, but again failed to really capture the imagination of the public.

Speedway's popularity never waned through the 1960s/70s, in fact the Aces won many Championships and Cups within this period, with riders like Ivan Mauger and Peter Craven proving immensely popular and bringing global attention to Belle Vue.

The unfortunate decline that Belle Vue Zoological Gardens experienced during the 1960s, 70s and 80s meant that eventually the park had to close the majority of its attractions and the once great resort was broken up piece by piece and sold off to the highest bidder. This was a tragedy for the area, which lost jobs and perhaps more importantly a focal point for its community.

So many sporting achievements are now relegated to memory. Ghosts of wrestlers and boxers haunt the site of the Kings Hall, searching for the sound of the fans that had loved them. But there is still some light in the fact that both speedway and greyhound racing still take place within reach of the original Belle Vue site. Although both remain popular, the long-gone days of the thirties and fourties may never be matched, but their memory will never be forgotten.

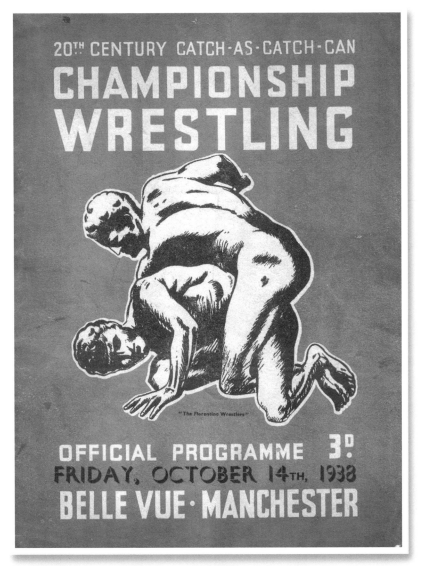

20TH CENTURY CATCH-AS-CATCH-CAN
CHAMPIONSHIP
WRESTLING

"The Florentine Wrestlers"

OFFICIAL PROGRAMME 3D.
FRIDAY, OCTOBER 14TH, 1938
BELLE VUE·MANCHESTER

The first wrestling contest took place in the Kings Hall on the 15 December 1930 and quickly began to draw large crowds. During the 1930s, the promotion of wrestling at Belle Vue was taken over by Miss Kathleen Look, who was the only female promoter in the country. She was married to E.O. Spence, the Belle Vue Speedway Manager at the time. Later in the 1940s, husband and wife team Jessie and Dick Rodgers promoted the sport.

One of the most recognised British grapplers ever, Giant Haystacks, was born in Camberwell Green, London. He stood 6'11 tall and weighed a massive 45-stone at his heaviest. The feud between Haystacks and Big Daddy is legendary and was watched by television audiences of up to 10 million on Saturday afternoons.

Price 6d.

GREYHOUND
Racing Association Ltd.
BELLE VUE, MANCHESTER

OPENING
MEETING
JULY 24TH, 1926
At 7-30 p.m.

SIX RACES
Prizes for Each Event—First £10 ; Second £5.

Judges :
Mr. O. A. CRITCHLEY, Major L. LYNE DIXSON, Mr. L. O. BROWN.
Timekeeper : Mr. E. WILKINSON.
Paddock Steward and Starter : Mr. W. SMITH.
Racing Secretary : Mr. MURRAY WILSON.

 The name of any dog unable to compete in a race will
be shown on the blackboard in each enclosure.

ALLIED NEWSPAPERS LTD., Printers, Withy Grove, Manchester.

The front cover of the program from the opening race meeting at Belle Vue in 1926. Greyhound racing at Belle Vue became a Manchester pastime over the years. As with almost everything Belle Vue did, the meetings became world famous and hugely popular.

FIRST RACE

¼ Mile.

7-30 p.m.

Colours.

1—Mr. W. R. Stewart .... r.d. **MISTLEY** (Jack-in-Office—Duck) .... Red 6/1

2—Lady Nash .... bd. & w.d. **PARAMETER** (Great Form—
Littleworth Lament) Blue 10/1

3—Mr. Charles Munn. Jnr. ..... r. or f.d. **CRYPTOGRAM** (Three Speed—
Magical Maid IV.) White 10/1

4—Mr. John Wanamaker .... bd.d. **OLD BEAN** (Wingle—Washover) .... Green 2/1

5—Mrs. Reginald Foster .... br.d. **AIR HAWK** (Hawklike—Air Combat) ...... Black 3/1

6—Mr. J. C. M. Kerslake .... bk.d. **HAPPY ACCEPTANCE** (Jasper—
Happy Coming) Orange 10/1

7—Mrs. Marshall Roberts .... f.d. **SUDBOURNE STIFF** (Hawklike—
Silvery Brook) Red & White 10/1

1ST MISTLEY - 2ND OLD BEAN - 3RD SUDBOORNE STIFF
8L - HEAD   TIME 25.00

SECOND RACE

The Stanley Course (500 yds.)

7-55 p.m.

Colours.

1—Miss Mary Astor Paul .... f.d. **MIGHTY** (Happy Bertie—Molly XI.) .... Red 2/1

2—Miss Constance Talmadge .... r.d. **PHILOSOPHER** (Derringer—Fantasy) .... Blue 10/1

3—Mrs. J. C. King .... f.d. **FAIRLY KEEN** (Admiral's Echo—
Wild Iris) White 5/1

4—Mrs. Marshall Roberts .... f.d. **LOPEX** (Admiral's Echo—Wild Iris) ...... Green 10/1

5—Mr. A. R. Tozer .... bd.b. **AFTER TIME** (Barr-na-Maidne—
Lockspit Lady) Black 10/1

6—Mr. P. M. Stewart .... bd.d. **BANNOCKBURN** (Fine Fight—
Air Combat) Orange 10/1

7—Lord Stanley .... bd.b. **EMERALD BROOCH** (Skeets—
Vicious Ada) Red & White 3/1

1ST BANNOCKBURN - 2ND MIGHTY - 3RD EMERALD BROOCH
        1L   3L   TIME 28.80

A part of the programme for the very first Greyhound Race meeting that took place in Belle Vue on 24 July 1926. Mistley, ironically the first dog listed, went on to win that race and so cement her place in history, all at 6/1!

Another wonderful image showing action from the first ever meeting held at Belle Vue in 1926. It is interesting to note the "hare" nearest to the camera. In the early days of the sport, a slow hare was used in order to draw the runners away from the inner rail. You can also see the Judges' box on the inside of the track.

elle Vue greyhound stadium became the ird dog track in Greater Manchester to be t by fire in nine days. Police stated that ere was no evidence to link the blazes d the mystery remains to this day. The tensive damage to the facilities are own in this image.

The burnt out Tote board at Belle Vue after fire ripped through the stadium. Electricians and engineers battled against time and horrendous weather to ensure that the "show" went on.

At the end of 1929, with more than thirty racecourses now operating in Britain, members of the Greyhound Racing Association committee were invited, with other sportsmen of standing and experience, to form the National Greyhound Racing Club, which became effective on 1 January 1928. This organisation was formed in order to protect the interests of the public by ensuring that greyhound racing on all tracks would be conducted honourably, and in the best traditions of the sport.

Due to the continuing popularity of Greyhound Racing, Belle Vue invested £30,000 in a new stand during the 1970s.

Greyhound racers Fever Maid, left, and Silver Circle, right, at Belle Vue dog track pictured at a time when English Heritage were trying to protect sporting venues in Manchester.

Queen Elizabeth II on a visit to Belle Vue in 1961. Right, Honorary Colonel of the Duke of Lancaster's Own Yeomanry bows as he greets the Queen on her arrival at Belle Vue Stadium.

Prince Philip leaves the stadium with Major General A. Read after his visit to the Armex 69 exhibition at Belle Vue. Army exhibitions such as this were a frequent and popular way of utilising Belle Vue's facilities.

This image shows the last moments of the Youth Festival at Belle Vue. Children always contributed much to the reputation of the park. From 1887 the old athletics ground was used for the annual Manchester and Salford schools' sports day.

After losing his Flyweight titles, Jackie Brown attempted a comeback as a Bantamweight, and his title challenge to stable companion Johnny King at Belle Vue on the 30 May 1937 was an eagerly awaited battle.

Jock McAvoy with a superb knock-out win to end his British Middleweight Championship fight with Archie Sexton in the Kings Hall, Belle Vue. The 1920s were a great time for boxing in Manchester, and Belle Vue became one of the best venues in Europe. Post-war, the appeal of boxing in the Kings Hall dipped, but there were notable exceptions, like the televised World-title bout between Willie Pastrano and Terry Downes in 1964.

Muhammad Ali is ushered through the large crowd at the Ideal Homes Exhibition staged at Belle Vue. Over the years, the park was a site of many exhibitions and, until the redevelopment of G-Mex in the 1980s, was Manchester's primary site for such events.

Local boxers Jonjo Green and Alex Penarski beat the crowds to meet former World Heavyweight Champion Muhammad Ali when he was a guest at the M.E.N Ideal Home Exhibition at Belle Vue.

Speedway

Mention speedway to an enthusiast of the sport and you will be regaled with tales of danger, high speed and endless thrills. Riders such as Frank "the Red Devil" Varney, Peter "Mighty Atom" Craven and James "Indian" Allen became legends as they tore around the Belle Vue track on powerful motor-cycles.

Speedway as a sport originated in Australia during the early part of the 20th Century. By the mid 1920s the sport was booming in the north of England and new tracks were appearing all over the region. The first known "dirt track racing" event to take place in Manchester was on 28 July 1928 when the late Johnnie Hoskins organised a meeting at Kirkmanshulme Lane that pitted five leading Australian riders against five of their British counterparts.

John Henry Iles spotted the potential of speedway and purchased a controlling interest in the North Manchester Motor Club. Part of the deal was that Iles would provide the club with a dirt racing track within Belle Vue Zoological Gardens for a minimum of five years. He built a state of the art stadium, which opened in March of 1929.

The "Aces", as Belle Vue's speedway team became known, earned a reputation as a formidable outfit made up of brave and entertaining riders. Without doubt the Aces were amongst Britain's best teams and continuously pulled huge crowds in excess of 30,000 into the Belle Vue stadium.

Perhaps Belle Vue's finest ever team was the one that won four consecutive League Championship titles, five National Trophies and four ACU Cups between 1933 and 1937. So dominant were the Aces during these glorious years that the team was often compared to the Busby Babes in terms of talent, ability and excitement. The team contained all-time greats such as Eric Langton, Frank Varey, Max Grosskreutz and Bill Kitchen, names to make any speedway fan jealous!

Not even the outset of war could defeat the Aces. Between 1939 and 1945, Belle Vue staged an incredible 170 senior meetings thus giving much needed entertainment to those affected by the horrors of wartime England. The management at Belle Vue also made a valuable contribution to the war effort by setting up a facility within the stadium where fans could donate blood to the St. John Ambulance.

The post-war years saw a continued growth in popularity for the sport as more teams came into existence both locally and globally. The Aces cemented their place amongst the very best with yet more National League and National Trophy titles.

For eleven years, from 1941 and 1952, the Belle Vue Aces had a female manager, Alice Hart. She eventually left the position after doing an amazing job of keeping speedway alive during the war-years. Johnnie Hoskins, who took over in 1952, always had a keen eye for new sports and forms of entertainment and was responsible for the introduction of Stock car racing to Belle Vue.

The fifties and sixties were full of incident for the Aces. Peter Craven, perhaps the finest ever rider in speedway, lit up the Belle Vue stadium week in week out with his electrifying riding and bravery. His tragic death in 1963 was a huge loss to speedway, though his achievements and personality will live forever in the hearts of fans worldwide.

Dent Oliver, a former rider, returned to Belle Vue in 1967 as Manager. He implemented a complete change in policy and with the introduction of Monday night training schools, ensured a steady supply of local riders for years to come. In fact, so many good riders took part in these sessions that the decision was made to form a separate team that would allow these youngsters to compete at a high level. The Belle Vue Colts raced for the first time in 1968 in the newly formed 2nd Division and achieved a tremendous double of League and Cup titles in their first season.

Although the Hyde Road Stadium is most famous for speedway, it was also used for a variety of different functions. Football, athletics, military exhibitions, stockcar racing and American football all took place within the wooden walls of Belle Vue.

Following the untimely closure of Belle Vue in the 1980s, the Speedway Stadium was sold to the British Car Auction Group. The final event to be held at the stadium was a stock car meet held on 14 November 1987, shortly before the stadium was demolished. The demise of the stadium left the Aces without a home, but fortunately, they were able to shift the club over to the Greyhound Stadium, ironically where they had started life in 1929.

A typically thrilling image from a speedway meeting inside the Belle Vue stadium in 1947. From left to right are: Wally Lloyd, Geoff Pymar and Lionel van Praal. After the war had finished, speedway experienced an upsurge in popularity and stadiums were once again packed to the rafters with excited spectators.

The Belle Vue squad of the mid thirties, pictured after their fourth consecutive National League triumph in 1936. Back row (left to right) are: Bill Kitchen, Max Grosskreutz, Oliver Langton, Stanley Dobson, Tommy Price, Joe Abbott, Bob Harrison and Frank Varey. Seated in front is captain Eric Langton. Stanley Dobson was christened "Acorn" after someone pointed out that his head was shaped like one! He was a vital part of the legendary Belle Vue team of the early 1930s who won five League titles in six years and also contained such greats as Frank Varey and Eric Langton. Dobson is remembered as a fearless rider who lived for the sport. Stanley once described his favourite aftershave as petrol and diesel!

Speedway legend Jack Parker gives his autograph to some lucky fans at the Belle Vue speedway track. Once described as the "champion of champions", Parker was certainly amongst the best riders in the history of the sport. He was one of the first Englishmen to challenge the supremacy of the visiting Australian riders. Parker amassed an incredible number of titles during his career in motorsport. In fact, he became so dominant in match races that the British Match Race Championship Golden Helmet was known as "Parker's Pension".

Some of the most memorable names in the history of Belle Vue speedway lined for this photograph in 1933. From left to right are: Eric Langton, Max Grosskreut "Bronco" Dixon, Bob Harrison, Frank Va and Bill Kitchen. Eric Langton was an ev present and vital member of the great Belle Vue teams during the 30s and 40s Born in Leeds in 1907, his career began before the start of British speedway as hugely talented road racer and trials ric He quickly adapted to the new sport an and became a much-feared competitor. Added to his racing talent was the amaz technical knowledge possessed by Lang and his brother Oliver. Together they pioneered many ideas such as using lig machines and different riding technique

Bill Kitchen (nearest the camera) with Wally Lloyd outside him, pictured in 1948. Kitchen was a great rider and hugely successful in speedway, winning countless races and trophies. He became a familiar face at Belle Vue, and was a rider that fans loved to hate.

Dent Oliver (left) pictured in 1948 with Louis Lawson (right). These two riders were part of the all-conquering Belle Vue team of the late forties who captured the National League Title time and again. They were compared with the Busby Babes in terms of talent and impact.

Bill Kitchen in Wembley colours with Wally Lloyd outside him. The Wembley team were a dominant force in speedway and were historically the Belle Vue team's main rival on a national level. Bill Kitchen rode with the Aces team, which included Langton, Varey, Abbott, Charles, Grosskreutz, Harrison, Gregory and Dixon.

Belle Vue "Aces" in 1969 (left to right): Chris Pusey, Bill Powell, Norman Nevitt, Dave Hemus, Ivan Mauger, Soren Sjosten and Tommy Roper (on bike). Chris Pusey was known throughout the sport as the Polka Dot Kid because of the highly individual helmet and leathers he wore in the late 1960s at a time when most riders still sported all-black leathers. He rode for the Aces from 1967 to 1974, a golden age for the club who won a straight hat-trick of British League titles.

Belle Vue's Soren Sjoston showing the typical dashing style that made him a popular and successful rider in the later 1960s. Speedway was and still is a truly international sport that attracts fans an competitors from every part of the globe.

During the 1950s, Speedway had become a well-established and popular sport with its own national organisation, a large following and good coverage in the press. Building on this success, promoters such as Johnnie Hoskins looked for other ways of using the numerous stadiums and tracks that had popped up all over the country.

Stock car racing, shown above, had been taking place for some time in America and its potential as an exciting sport was quickly spotted. Although many of those involved in speedway mocked the new sport, it was a great spectacle and thousands of fans were flocking to newly-built tracks to witness the action. Belle Vue staged its first stock car meeting on 16 June 1954.

As the sport grew in popularity, it became more organised. In August 1955, Hoskins organised a one race "World Championship" which was won by Jerry Woltowicz. Belle Vue continued to host the Championship and stock car racing continued to attract good crowds and sponsors were keen to be associated with the sport.

Peter Craven was born in Liverpool on June 1934. Peter's elder brother Brian started the speedway "bug" in the family when he progressed from cycle speedway, a popular sport at the time, to "real" speedway in 1949. A day after his 16th birthday, Peter went along to the track and had his first ride, promptly crashing the bike and sustaining a concussion. Luckily for fans of the sport he didn't let that put him off for long! He managed to combine racing for Belle Vue and completing his national service. During 1954 he made 25 appearances and topped the score chart at Belle Vue with 200 points. That year he also qualified for his first Wembley World Final. A year later Craven stormed back to Wembley and took the World Championship. As a World Champion at the start of the 1963 season, Craven was automatically selected as a challenger for the Golden Helmet Match race title, which was held at the time by his old rival Ove Fundin. Peter finally defeated Fundin in the decider. Within a few days of the World Final, Craven was racing at Meadowbank, the Provincial League Champions. After three brilliant wins, he crashed heavily in the fourth outing, after trying to avoid another fallen rider. He eventually succumbed to serious head injuries and died a few days later. As a consequence of his death, Britain lost its most consistent post-war rider and its only serious challenger to the foreign and overseas domination of the sport.

Aces rider Alan Wilkinson pictured with his bike at Belle Vue. A hugely popular rider, Wilkinson was skipper of the Belle Vue team until he was involved in a serious accident in July 1978 which left him confined to a wheelchair. He garners incredible respect from all those involved with the sport.

Arnold Haley trying on an Aces bib for the first time after his signing from Sheffield. He is pictured with Chris Morton and team manager Eric Boocock.

Alan Wilkinson seen here in action as a Belle Vue Ace. He was a key member of the team and represented the Aces as club captain.

Swedish ace of the Belle Vue team, Soren Sjosten pictured here in the early 1970s. The Swedish rider was the FIM World Paris Champion in 1974.

Ivan Mauger (right) with the British League Speedway Riders' Championship trophy. Mauger arrived at Belle Vue in 1969 and the legendary Kiwi quickly showed a steely single-minded determination to his racing. He led the Aces to three Championships and a Knockout Cup win in the late 60s and early 70s before moving to Devon. He remains the only rider to win three consecutive FIM Championship Gold Medals. In 1970, two men in the USA promised to have his bike covered in gold if he won a third consecutive medal, which he promptly did. In an incredible career he won six World Speedway Championships, three World Longtrack Championships, four World Team Championships, four European Championships, one Intercontinental Championship, two British-Nordic Championships and four British Championships.

Belle Vue Aces with their British League trophies. Pictured from left to right are: Stuart Bamforth (promoter), Peter Carr, Rod Hunter, Chris Morton (on bike), Larry Ross, Andy Smith, Peter Raven (kneeling), Jimmy McMillan, Louis Carr, Peter Collins and team manager Ian Thomas. Peter Collins was born in 1954 and began riding motorcycles on his father's farm as a child. He started attending speedway races at the Hyde Road Stadium and by the age of 16 was competing at grass track meets. It was during this period that he came to the attention of Belle Vue and they signed him for the Aces. By 1972, Peter was a full-time Belle Vue racer and quickly became one of the team's star riders. Without doubt his most impressive achievement was the Individual World Speedway Championship. He won this title at the Slaski Stadium at Chorozow Katowice, Poland, in 1976. Ironically, he became the first British rider to win this title since Peter Craven, his predecessor at Belle Vue.

This wonderful image shows that Belle Vue's legendary riders will always have a place in the hearts of speedway fans. To commemorate the Golden Jubilee, Belle Vue organised a parade for some of the great riders of the fourties and fifties.

A recent crop of Belle Vue riders followed their predecessors at the Golden Jubilee celebrations. The old riders, who used to light up Belle Vue Speedway Stadium, have cemented a place in the history of the region and its sporting heroes.

Conclusion

Attendances at Belle Vue had been falling gradually since the early 1960s. For a variety of reasons, the park became dated and as other competitors began to emerge, the number of people visiting Belle Vue really started to decline. It soon became clear that the future of the park as a centre for entertainment and leisure would have to be looked at carefully.

During the late 1960s in particular, the lack of customers hit Belle Vue severely. The drop in revenue led in turn to a complete lack of adequate investment in the park. At a time when re-development was crucial, nothing was done and Belle Vue began to sink into disarray. Cutbacks were made, staff lost their jobs and many of Belle Vue's most famous features were gradually broken down, sold off and even destroyed. This disastrous process left a massive gap in the region that has never been filled.

The "Bobs", that iconic symbol of Belle Vue's past glory, was demolished in 1971, the firework displays which had thrilled generations of visitors ceased in 1969 and the Scenic Railway was not used after 1975. Attendances at the zoo were affected by the opening of competitors such as Blackpool Zoo in 1973 and Knowsley Safari Park in 1971. These new competitors had a much more modern approach than Belle Vue, whose once cutting edge practices were now looking dated.

Although attendances at the zoo experienced a brief renaissance in 1975 and 1976, the economic pressures placed upon it had become too great a burden to carry. With costs escalating, and many of the buildings becoming more and more dilapidated, things quickly became extremely bleak. Finally, in November 1971, the zoo was permanently closed and many staff-members lost their jobs.

Many of the animals were transferred to new homes, but there were a number who could not deal with such a change and sadly had to be put down. The last animal remained at the zoo until February 1979. "Ellie-May", the elephant, was eventually found a new home, but as she was led out of her pen, she refused to enter her transport. Overnight, she developed pneumonia and a serious heart complaint. Eventually, staff realised that it would be better for her to be put down, and she died in her home, the last of the Belle Vue animals.

Following the closure of the zoo, futile attempts were made to retain and expand on the remaining features, but they had little impact on the dwindling popularity of the park. More and more of the original attractions of Belle Vue were slowly disappearing as money ran out. Even the catering and entertainment suites, which had remained reasonably successful, began to suffer and were eventually closed. The Amusement Park was rented out to Mr Wadbrooke, who ran it only on weekends and holidays.

Trust House Forte decided that the remaining profitable elements of the site did not justify keeping Belle Vue open and began to look at ways to sell the entire site. By 1980, they had decided on a scheme whereby a mixture of housing and industrial sites would replace entertainment. In January 1981, the majority of the site was sold to the Espley Tyas Development Group, who agreed to honour all remaining contracts in the Exhibition Halls for 18 months. They also left the Kings Hall in the control of Trust House Forte until the end of the Christmas Circus in 1981/82.

These announcements heralded a storm of protests. Two separate action groups were formed and a petition containing 50,000 signatures was presented to the City Council. Despite massive oppositions, the sale went ahead, and in September 1981, much of the remaining site was demolished. The Speedway Stadium and the Bowling Centre were saved, but a huge amount of features were resigned to Manchester's history.

In 1983, the Exhibition Halls were taken over by Mullet Ltd, who had some initial success in their attempts to revive this part of Belle Vue, but the opening of the G-Mex in 1986 was a severe blow and led directly to the sale of the site to the British Car Auction Group, who demolished the remaining buildings and replaced them with a large car auction centre.

Although there are still some remnants of Belle Vue's former glory in existence, they are unfortunately few and far between. What was once a place of fun and almost unlimited entertainment has become an industrial and residential area. For those who never experienced Belle Vue, it seems almost impossible that a place capable of hosting over 150,000 people in a single day and 2 million in a year existed right on their doorstep for over a hundred glorious years.

But there it was, giving people of the North an opportunity to see animals from the far corners of the earth, to eat great food, drink, dance in the sumptuous surroundings of the Ballroom, listen to wonderful music in the Kings Hall, ride on roller coasters, watch sport and experience the sights and sounds of the legendary circus.

Belle Vue is missed by its visitors and generations of local people who spent their whole working lives in the park. From zookeepers to refreshment staff, fathers to sons, hundreds of men and women enjoyed helping the park to deliver its legendary mix of wonder and amazement to its guests.

When it closed, Belle Vue left a gaping hole in the heart of the region that has never been completely replaced. It gave people a focal point, something to be proud of, a place where they could take their families and be sure of a great day out at a reasonable cost.

This is an image of the main entrance to Belle Vue that was situated on Hyde Road. This was the entrance through which so many thousands of happy customers passed over the years. The turnstiles were rebuilt in 1957 by the architects Tom Hayes and Partners who were associated with many of the improvements to the park undertaken after 1956.

Rubble that was the Kings Hall. The wooden structure which was the home of the Belle Vue Circus for so many years and was also used for wrestling, boxing and brass band competitions eventually succumbed to the pressures put upon it by the changing times and was demolished to make way for housing and industrial buildings.

Matt Kelly, retired Head Keeper, returned to Belle Vue in order to protest against the demolition of the site. Despite heroic efforts on his and so many other people's part, the decline of the zoo proved unstoppable and the site was eventually demolished.

Acknowledgements

Our thanks firstly go to the *Manchester Evening News* for use of their incredible pictorial archive that inspired us to write this book and equally our thanks go to Wayne Ankers.

We also want to thank Jane Foster at Chethams Library for her willingness to help us search through all their Belle Vue information. The Chethams archive is arguably the best collection of Belle Vue information, stretching all the way back to the Jennison era.

Other images of family days out were provided by Jan Hollins and her father James, thank you for granting us access to your family photos. Manchester Central Library's Local History Department was invaluable as a resource and the staff were always extremely helpful, many thanks.

Heartfelt thanks also go to David Gray at The Monastery of St Francis & Gorton Trust. David shared his memories of working at the Great Ape House in the final days of Belle Vue's history. He brought us into contact with Frank Rhodes and Marie Koudellas who also took time to look at the images in this book and helped to correct some of our information, thank you. Gorton Monastery is undergoing significant redevelopment and eventually an exhibition of Belle Vue will be held there.

We acknowledge the research and writing of Clive Bennet and David Barnaby, Frank Rhodes and Jill Cronin, C.H. Keeling, Robert Nicholls, Trevor James and Barry Stephenson and the amazing video footage of Roy Nichol. The information and collection of memories captured in each of their titles allows Belle Vue to continue in some small measure.

We hope that this book allows the visitors and workers of Belle Vue to remember their time spent in one of Manchester's most magical places. Belle Vue Zoological Gardens is largely consigned to history but memories allow it to be a living history.